SPORTS INJURIES:
HOW TO PREVENT, DIAGNOSE, & TREAT

HOCKEY

Sports Injuries:
How to Prevent, Diagnose, & Treat

- Baseball
- Basketball
- Cheerleading
- Equestrian
- Extreme Sports
- Field
- Field Hockey
- Football
- Gymnastics
- Hockey
- Ice Skating
- Lacrosse
- Soccer
- Track
- Volleyball
- Weight Training
- Wrestling

SPORTS INJURIES: HOW TO PREVENT, DIAGNOSE, & TREAT

HOCKEY

JOHN WRIGHT

MASON CREST PUBLISHERS

www.masoncrest.com

Mason Crest Publishers Inc.
370 Reed Road
Broomall, PA 19008
(866) MCP-BOOK (toll free)
www.masoncrest.com

First printing

1 2 3 4 5 6 7 8 9 10

Library of Congress Cataloging-in-Publication Data on file
at the Library of Congress

ISBN 1-59084-634-6

Series ISBN 1-59084-625-7

Editorial and design by
Amber Books Ltd.
Bradley's Close
74–77 White Lion Street
London N1 9PF
www.amberbooks.co.uk

Project Editor: Michael Spilling
Design: Graham Curd
Picture Research: Natasha Jones

Printed and bound in the Hashemite Kingdom of Jordan

PICTURE CREDITS
Corbis: 6, 8, 10, 11, 12, 17, 18, 20, 24, 26, 28, 32, 34, 35, 36, 37, 38, 42,
48, 50, 52, 53, 54, 56; **©EMPICS**: 14, 15, 21, 22, 23, 45, 59.

FRONT COVER: All ©EMPICS, except Corbis (br).

ILLUSTRATIONS: Courtesy of Amber Books except:
Bright Star Publishing plc: 40, 44, 46, 47;
Tony Randell: 31.

CONTENTS

Foreword   6

History   8

Visualizing Success   18

Warm-Ups and Conditioning   24

Protective Equipment   32

Injuries and Treatment   38

Careers in Hockey   50

Glossary   60

Further Information   62

Index   64

Foreword

Sports Injuries: How to Prevent, Diagnose, and Treat is a seventeen-volume series written for young people who are interested in learning about various sports and how to participate in them safely. Each volume examines the history of the sport and the rules of play; it also acts as a guide for prevention and treatment of injuries, and includes instruction on stretching, warming up, and strength training, all of which can help players avoid the most common musculoskeletal injuries. *Sports Injuries* offers ways for readers to improve their performance and gain more enjoyment from playing sports, and young athletes will find these volumes informative and helpful in their pursuit of excellence.

Sports medicine professionals assigned to a sport that they are not familiar with can also benefit from this series. For example, a football athletic trainer may need to provide medical care for a local gymnastics meet. Although the emergency medical principles and action plan would remain the same, the athletic trainer could provide better care for the gymnasts after reading a simple overview of the principles of gymnastics in *Sports Injuries*.

Although these books offer an overview, they are not intended to be comprehensive in the recognition and management of sports injuries. The text helps the reader appreciate and gain awareness of the common injuries possible during participation in sports. Reference material and directed readings are provided for those who want to delve further into the subject.

Written in a direct and easily accessible style, *Sports Injuries* is an enjoyable series that will help young people learn about sports and sports medicine.

Susan Saliba, Ph.D., National Athletic Trainers' Association Education Council

The national teams of Russia (in red) and Germany meet at the Olympic Games in 1994.

History

Ice hockey, simply known as hockey in the United States, is the world's fastest team sport. Players have been clocked at 29 miles per hour (47 km/h), while the puck speeds at more than 100 miles per hour (160 km/h).

A favorite sport in cold climates, hockey has recently undergone a boom in popularity in all regions of the country, thanks to artificial ice rinks and indoor arenas. The game's exciting combination of speed, power skating, and agility has won over thousands of new players and millions of fans. The sport developed out of the English game of bandy, which is played on ice with a stick and small hard ball. Bandy was first played in about 1800, but mild English winters caused the game to decline at the beginning of the twentieth century, although it is still played by Scandinavians and Russians.

It was in Canada that bandy was transformed into hockey during the winter of 1853, when soldiers in a garrison decided to replace the ball with a disk-shaped block of wood for their games on a frozen lake. Fifteen years later, on March 3, 1875, the first indoor game was played, with nine players on each team, in front of spectators at the Victoria Rink in Montreal.

Two McGill University students, W. F. Robertson and R. F. Smith, devised the game's first rules in 1879. They took many of them from rugby and field hockey. They also introduced the first rubber **puck**, which was square, and set the number of players on a team at six (a goaltender, two backs, and three forwards).

Hockey begins with a face-off in the middle of the rink to see who can control a puck dropped by the referee. Play is also restarted with a face-off after a break in the action.

The McGill University Hockey Club was formed a year later as the first official club. From there, hockey quickly caught the public's imagination, and its popularity grew rapidly in Canada and the northeastern part of the United States.

A special incentive was introduced for the 1893–1894 season, when the Governor General of Canada, Lord Stanley of Preston, donated a cup to be given to the leading Canadian hockey club. Amateur teams throughout the country began to recruit good athletes to compete for the new Stanley Cup. In 1887, the Ontario Hockey Association was established to oversee amateur hockey, and, by 1896, the United States had a four-club United States Amateur Hockey League in New York City. The first game ended in a 15–0 victory by the St. Nicholas

Amateur hockey flourished in the first half of the twentieth century. This team from the Flour City Coal and Oil Company posed on the ice with their coaches in 1934.

GORDIE HOWE (1928–)

Called "Mr. Hockey," Gordie Howe played for five decades (1946–1980). Retiring at age fifty-two, he returned briefly in 1997 at age sixty-nine. He was the first player to score 1,000 major league points (goals and assists) in a career, ending with 1,850. He set NHL records for the most goals (801), games (1,767), and seasons (26); won the Hart Trophy for the most valuable player six times; and took six scoring titles. Noted for his toughness, he fractured his

Howe was 6 ft 1 in (1.85 m) and weighed 205 lbs (93 kg), letting him overpower most opponents.

skull in 1950 and was told not to play again, but he was back the next year as the league's scoring leader. Howe took part in the Detroit Red Wings camp at the age of sixteen, and then played for them at right wing from 1946 to 1971. Next he played for the Houston Aeros (1973–1977) alongside his two sons, Mark and Marty, and moved with them to the Hartford (now New England) Whalers (1977–1980).

"You've got to love what you're doing," Howe said. "If you love it, you can overcome any handicap or the soreness of all the aches and pains, and continue to play for a long, long time."

The U.S. Olympic Ice Hockey Team controls the puck against the U.S.S.R. at the 1972 games in Sapporo, Japan. The Americans took the silver medal behind the champion Russians.

Skating Club over the Brooklyn Skating Club. Colleges also began accepting the game as an important addition to their sports calendars.

PROFESSIONAL HOCKEY

Hockey then went professional, the first teams being organized in the early twentieth century in Canada and, in the United States, Michigan and Pennsylvania. The National Hockey Association was founded in Canada in 1909, and three years later professional teams were competing for the Stanley Cup. In 1917, the National Hockey League (NHL), an outgrowth of the association, was founded in Canada with four teams. By 1924, it had added U.S. clubs, eventually expanding to a total of ten teams. The sport also received a boost when it was played unofficially at the 1920 Olympic Games in Antwerp, Belgium. Strangely, this took place in the summer, and it was the Canadians who won gold, beating three other teams from the United States, Czechoslovakia, and Sweden.

In the late 1920s, the game became faster paced and soared in popularity when the forward pass was made legal in all three zones of the ice. By 1942, the NHL had been pared down to six strong (and still familiar) teams: the Boston Bruins, Chicago Black Hawks, Detroit Red Wings, Montreal Canadiens, New York Rangers, and Toronto Maple Leafs. Until 1967, these six teams played to win the Prince of Wales Trophy for the league championship, and the four best teams faced off for the Stanley Cup. The league doubled in size in 1967, with the original teams making up the Eastern Division and the newcomers comprising the Western Division. Expansion continued, and the 2002–2003 season had thirty teams. The four leading teams now have playoffs, which lead to a final best-of-seven series for the cup.

HOCKEY GOES WORLDWIDE

Hockey was introduced into Europe in the first half of the twentieth century. Canadian students in England began playing it in 1902 at the Prince's Skating Club in London, inspiring the formation of a five-team league. It was the British who invented the artificial rinks where the ice is frozen electrically. The International Ice Hockey Federation (IIHF) was formed in 1908, and a year later field hockey players introduced the game to Czechoslovakia. Bandy players first played the new game in Sweden in 1920, in Norway in 1934, and in the Soviet Union in 1946.

Canadian teams dominated the early years of Olympic hockey, taking six of the first seven gold medals—Great Britain won the other. In 1956, the Soviet Union became preeminent, winning the first of its seven gold medals. Canada equaled that record by taking gold in 2002, defeating the United States 5–2. The United States

Catherine Granato scoops the puck away for the U.S. Women's Ice Hockey Team playing Finland at the 1998 Olympic Games in Nagano, Japan. The U.S. team upset Canada for the gold medal.

has won only twice—in 1960 and 1980—but, in each case, spectacular upsets over favored nations led to an upswing in participation by young players throughout the country and a greatly expanded number of hockey fans. The U.S. women's Olympic hockey team also found fame, winning the first ever women's competition at the 1998 games at Nagano, Japan, by defeating the Canadians twice, 7–4 and 3–1. The Canadians got revenge in the 2002 games, defeating the Americans 3–2.

The Hockey Hall of Fame was established in 1943 and completed its own building in 1961 within the Canadian National Exhibition grounds in Toronto. In 1993, it moved to a new $35 million facility in downtown Toronto, drawing more than 500,000 visitors in its first year.

WAYNE GRETZKY (1961–)

Known as the greatest player in history, when Wayne Gretzky retired in 1999 after twenty years in the NHL, he held or shared sixty-one records. He holds the all-time scoring record of 2,857 points, with 894 goals and 1,963 assists in 1,487 career games. The only player in NHL history to score more than 200 points in one season, he led the league in scoring nine times and was named the most valuable player nine times.

Born in Brantford, Ontario, Canada, he began his career in 1978 with the Indianapolis Racers of the World Hockey Association. That same year, he was traded to the Edmonton Oilers, whom he led to four Stanley Cup championships (1984, 1985, 1987, 1988), and was traded to the Los Angeles Kings in 1989, when he became the NHL's highest-ever scorer. In recognition of his achievements, Gretzky's jersey number has now been retired by the league—number 99 will never again be worn by an NHL player.

Gretzky was inducted into the Hockey Hall of Fame seven months after he retired.

BASIC HOCKEY RULES

Hockey is played on ice by two teams of six players each: a goaltender to protect the goal, a center, left and right wings who skate near their sides of the rink, and left and right defensemen who defend near their goal. The players skate holding a wooden stick to control and pass the puck, which they shoot at the opponent's goal.

The game lasts for three twenty-minute periods, with a fifteen-minute break between each period. If the game is tied at the end, a five-minute "sudden death" overtime is played, and the first team to score wins.

THE RINK

An NHL rink is 85 feet (26 m) wide and 200 feet (61 m) long, and has rounded corners. Surrounding the rink, to protect the fans, are plastic or fiberglass boards 42 inches (1.06 m) high, and there is often shatterproof glass above the boards. The rink is divided by blue lines into three sections: the neutral zone in the center; the defending zone, where a team protects its goal; and the attacking zone, the opponent's goal. Face-off circles are also drawn on the ice in nine positions where the puck may be put into play by a referee or linesman.

THE GAME

The game begins with a face-off in the middle of the rink, with the referee dropping the puck between the opposing centers. Players on the team controlling the puck pass it down the rink and can score by directing it between the posts of their opponent's goal, as long as it completely passes the red goal line in front of the goal. The other team can intercept the puck at any time, and a player can "check" an opponent by making hard body contact with him to stop a pass or shot.

If a player draws a penalty, he must spend time in the penalty box, a bench located just off the ice. Five minutes are assessed for a major penalty, such as fighting or "spearing" (using the stick like a spear against an opponent), and two minutes for a minor one, such as tripping or holding. If a player is illegally denied a scoring opportunity, the referee may award a penalty shot in which that player alone moves the puck from the center toward the goalie, one-on-one.

Players wait at the face-off before the referee drops the puck to begin a game.

Visualizing Success

Imagination is a powerful force. We have all experienced the near reality of memory and daydreams, especially during quiet times free of outside distractions. This vivid imagery has become an important way of enhancing sports performance.

Hockey players and other athletes have turned positive mental control into a regular program to improve their self-confidence, motivation, and performance. Skills can be reinforced and improved when a player imagines playing at a high level and achieving victory. Sports psychologists call this "**visualization**." Your coaches will set physical goals and help sharpen your skills on the ice, but you alone are in control of visualization and its many benefits.

A key benefit of visualization is the building of a positive self-image, important because negative thoughts have been proven to cause not only defeat, but also injuries. It is important to imagine yourself being in control on the ice and doing your best to play safely and have fun.

REHEARSING IN THE MIND

Train your mind regularly, especially during the season. Spend ten to fifteen minutes a day away from the rink and three to five minutes before training or a game. A relaxed state makes you more receptive to mental imagery. It is obviously easier to relax at home in moments when you can totally concentrate, as in the bathtub or in bed

Mental imagery can allow a player to "see" himself making the best plays during a game. Such a picture in the mind builds a positive self-image and improves performance.

The visualization technique should be intense, creating a clear picture that includes sounds, physical feelings, and emotions. Players should focus on their outstanding plays.

before falling asleep. A short pregame mental session is also possible, and hockey players practice "relaxed attention" during the break between periods or even while sitting in the penalty box. In this mental state, players are calm yet energized, so relaxed and confident that their actions on the ice seem to be almost automatic.

When visualizing yourself in a game, try to make the picture in your mind as clear as possible. See the colors of the uniforms, players scrambling after the face-off, the white nylon of the goal, and details of the rink; hear the blades scraping the ice, the crack of the stick on the puck, the referee's whistle, the massive thump

TACTICS AND STRATEGIES

The speed of hockey seems almost to defy measured tactics, but the best players can anticipate action down the ice and employ a variety of moves to adjust to the situation and to confuse the other side. Some of these moves include:

- Screening—Players on the attacking team will position themselves in front of the goaltender in order to screen or block the goalie's view of an upcoming shot.

- Deflection shot—Instead of taking a straight shot at the goal, which might be anticipated by a goalie, an attacking player shoots the puck to a nearby teammate, who quickly deflects it toward the goal from a different angle.

- Deke move—Deke is short for "decoy." Here an attacker fakes the direction of a pass or move by the movement of his or her stick or head and shoulders.

Players use many clever "deke" faking movements in order to outmaneuver opponents.

- Pulling the goalie—A team can gain an extra offensive player by moving the goalie to join the attack. This is a desperate ploy for a team facing defeat in the last minutes, and it leaves the goal open if the opponents control the puck.

as you check an opponent on the boards, the excited sounds of the crowd, and even your own breath; feel the uniform, your gloves grasping the stick, and the muscles in your legs moving as you skate to the goal. Note your emotions as you speed over the ice, maneuvering past the last defense for a clear shot at the goal—or, if you are the goalie, imagine yourself hunkering down to block a shot.

Reinforce your skills by adding mental images of particular movements of your body. Revive the memories of your best plays, such as your best backhand shot, a perfect assist to your teammate, or the strength in your shoulders as you body check your opponent's progress. Focus on the way you felt after an outstanding play and the approval you heard from the crowd. The more often you focus on success, the more often success will seem the normal situation.

A hockey variation for disabled players is sledge hockey. This action occurred between Norway and Japan at the 2002 Winter Paralympics in Salt Lake City, Utah.

HOCKEY TERMS

- **Body check**—Using the body to block the puck carrier, stopping an attack on the goal.
- **Changing on the fly**—Substituting players without stopping the game.
- **Clearing the puck**—Shooting the puck away from the front of the goal or out of the defending zone.

Hockey has a special language of its own. This attempted "stick check" ended in a tangle.

- **Face-off**—An action beginning play, when the referee drops the puck between the opposing centers.
- **Hat trick**—Three or more goals scored in one game by the same player.
- **Icing**—A rule violation whereby an offensive player shoots the puck from behind the center red line all the way across the opponent's goal line—unless, of course, it scores a goal. (The goal line extends across the rink and the goal itself sits on only a small part of it.)
- **Offsides**—A rule violation whereby an offensive player goes past the blue line into the attacking zone before the puck does.
- **Slap shot**—A hard shot taken by swinging the stick in a long sweeping motion.
- **Stick check**—Using the stick to take the puck away from opponents, with a poking, hooking, or sweeping motion.

Warm-Ups and Conditioning

Warming up before games is a good way to ensure your best performance and avoid injuries. The best hockey players maintain a flexible body to increase their range of movement, and this involves regular stretching exercises.

Stretching helps your blood flow and warms the muscles and **tendons**, loosening and relaxing them. This helps prevent injuries, which happen easily if muscles are tight. A short warm-up also increases your heart rate and pumps more oxygen into your **cardiovascular** system.

Hockey players always warm up before the face-off, but they have less pregame time on the ice than, say, a football player warming up on the field or a basketball player on the court. And exercising before coming into the arena is also difficult because of their skates. Even so, short stretching exercises—shoulder shrugs, waist bends, neck turns, knee lifts, and arm circles—can be done on the spot in the locker room before putting on the gear.

Once in the arena, you can continue to stretch when gliding around the ice:

• Bend one knee while keeping the other leg straight behind. Then switch to stretch the other leg.

Other exercises while gliding involve using the hockey stick:

Brett Hull of the St. Louis Blues does stretching exercises under the city's famous Gateway Arch. Warming up away from the arena is part of year-round conditioning.

A pregame warm-up on the ice allows a hockey player to loosen his muscles and provides an easy practice session. Stretching exercises can also be done in the locker room.

- Hold the stick with both hands behind the back and lift it away from the body.
- Raise the stick over the head and tilt the body to the right and left.
- Hold the stick in front and bend forward at the hips.

COOLING DOWN

You should also take time after a game for a cooling down period, which can be five minutes or less. The game is a physically demanding sport, which causes the muscles to pump blood to the heart, and these muscles will feel stiff or sore after the game because they still contain extra blood. Help muscles return more quickly to normal by stretching or walking around the dressing room immediately after coming off the ice. Players who sit down immediately after a game may feel dizzy or even faint.

It is important to follow a program of stretching and exercising each day during the season, even when no game or practice is scheduled. This will build up endurance against fatigue, which leads to many injuries. You can maintain flexibility and strength by first stretching to warm up and then doing **aerobic** exercises, such as running, swimming, push-ups, pull-ups, sit-ups, and jumping jacks. Even if you exercise for only twenty minutes three times a week, this will condition both your legs and upper body. If your fitness level is very good, extend your exercise sessions to an hour. You could also do weight training, but young players should avoid heavy weights, which may injure the **cartilage** where growth occurs.

EATING WELL

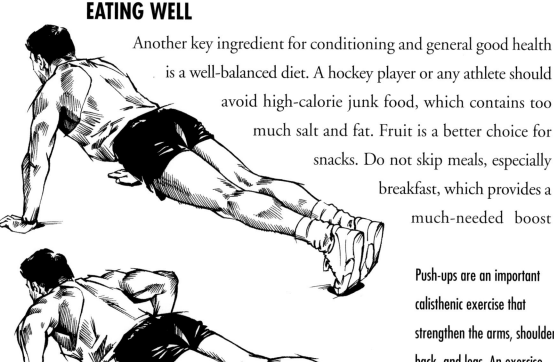

Another key ingredient for conditioning and general good health is a well-balanced diet. A hockey player or any athlete should avoid high-calorie junk food, which contains too much salt and fat. Fruit is a better choice for snacks. Do not skip meals, especially breakfast, which provides a much-needed boost

Push-ups are an important calisthenic exercise that strengthen the arms, shoulders, back, and legs. An exercise program builds up a player's strength and endurance.

of energy in the morning and should provide about one-third of your daily calorie intake. Complex carbohydrates should make up around 60 percent of your food each day because they provide fuel for your body. Good sources are found in such vegetables as peas and beans, and in fruit, bread, and pasta. Protein that builds muscles should comprise about 20 percent of your food intake, with the best sources being lean meats, low-fat fish, nuts, milk, and cheese. Another 20 percent should come from fat, which gives added energy and helps insulate against the cold; again, nuts, along with vegetable oil and margarine, are a good source.

Water is another important element for players. Dehydration during a game will lead to fatigue and injuries. Besides a loss of energy, the symptoms are muscle

Fitness is vital for a player because of hockey's rapid, extreme movements. Here a goaltender stretches to block a shot from Wayne Gretzky during a 1984 All-Star game.

TIPS ON EXERCISING

Any exercise session should take into account a player's fitness because it takes about six to eight weeks to get into top shape after beginning a conditioning program. Follow these five steps for the best results:

1. Start your program gradually, beginning with a workout of about twenty to thirty minutes, which can slowly be increased to an hour. Do not let yourself become fatigued during any session.

2. Warm up before each exercise period by stretching for ten to fifteen minutes first.

3. Exercise to your capacity to build up endurance, but do not overwork your body. If you are breathless and unable to carry on a conversation, reduce the level of intensity.

4. Mix the exercises to work on flexibility, strength, and the special movements required in hockey.

5. Establish a daily routine of warm-ups and exercise, both during the season and off season.

cramps and a light-headed or dizzy feeling. Players should avoid colas, coffee, and tea, all of which are high in caffeine and are also **diuretics**. Sports drinks are fine, but the best lubricant is plain water, which makes up 60 percent of the body's weight, helping to maintain a correct body temperature and to lubricate the joints. Fluids also let the circulatory system function efficiently and aid the lymph nodes in carrying away impurities. A proper amount of water is 1–2 quart (0.9–1.8 l) daily.

STRETCHING EXERCISES

The following simple exercises can be done in the dressing room before suiting up or as a daily program away from the rink. Start at the neck and work down. Do each stretch five times and hold for six to ten seconds.

NECK

1. Lean your head to the right toward your shoulder. Repeat, leaning toward the left shoulder.

2. Interlock your fingers behind your head, and pull it gently toward your chest.

3. Grab the back of your head with the right hand, and pull it gently forward to the right. Do the same with your left hand.

SHOULDERS

1. Make an exaggerated shrug, moving your shoulders upward with your arms at your sides. Let your shoulders drop, and move them in slow circles.

2. Hold your arms out at the sides and try to touch your palms together behind your back.

BACK

1. Lie on your back and grasp your knees, pulling them close to your chest.

2. Lie on your back with your arms outspread on the floor; turn your head to the right, then pull your right knee close to your chest and try to touch it to the floor on the left side. Repeat for the left knee.

CALF AND ACHILLES TENDON

1. Put your hands flat against a wall and position one foot in front of the other. Move your back leg farther from the wall, pressing the heel on the floor. Switch legs and repeat.

2. Stand 1 foot (30 cm) from the wall with one leg behind you, keeping both feet flat on the floor. Lean into the wall while keeping your back straight. Switch legs and repeat.

HAMSTRINGS

Stand about 1 foot (30 cm) from a wall and place your hands at shoulder height against the wall. Push against the wall with your back straight, then step back with your right leg, pressing the heel on the floor. Repeat for left leg.

Try this alternative hamstring stretch: sit on the ground with both legs in front. Bend the right knee and keep the right leg flat on the floor until the sole of the foot rests against the inside of your left knee. Then bend forward with your back straight. Repeat for left leg.

Protective Equipment

Hockey is an enjoyable sport, but there are many dangers on the ice. The hard flying puck, skates with sharp steel blades, the hockey stick's swinging blade and shaft, and collisions on the ice all cause a variety of injuries—and many more are prevented by the high-tech protective equipment worn by amateurs and professionals alike.

HELMET AND MOUTH GUARD

Hockey players at all levels are required to wear a helmet because a hard blow to the head by the puck or a stick could cause a serious injury, including a **concussion**. It is important that a player makes certain that the helmet fits perfectly, both for safety and comfort; it should fit snugly and not wiggle. The lightweight plastic helmet is lined with pads, at least $^5/_8$ inch (13 mm) thick, to absorb any impact; some models have an extra lining to increase comfort. All have holes on the sides for ventilation. In addition, helmets have either wire face masks, plastic face shields, or a combination of the two, to guard against injuries to the nose, jaw, teeth, and eyes. The wire versions, often made of stainless steel, cover all of the facial area and will not fog up like some face shields. The plastic

A face mask is one of the essential protective devices worn by a hockey goaltender. It offers safety from pucks flying at 100 miles per hour (160 km/h) and also provides open viewing from both sides.

shields cover the front of the face and offer a better overall view. Many do fog up, but some are now produced with a special coating that resists fogging. A combination face protector is available that has a plastic shield to guard the upper part of the face, including the eyes, and a wire mask below to protect the jaw and enable easier breathing. An extra safety item for the helmet is a pair of ear protectors, which also provide warmth.

A mouth guard should be worn to give more protection to the teeth, and it can also protect against concussions by softening blows to the head. Mouth guards are sold already formed and can then be made soft by heating so that the player can bite down and create an individual mold.

BOOTS

Hockey boots are usually made of a combination of leather and synthetic materials, and have heavy pads that also cover the ankles. The boots should be tight enough to cause no rubbing and to provide good stability. Players should always wear their hockey socks when trying on boots. Defensemen have stronger boots than offensive forwards because they will take more hits from hard shots.

A player in full protective equipment looks untouchable. The paddings, gloves, and boots help protect ice hockey players against injuries in this full-contact sport.

Hockey boots protect the ankles with pads. The skates are rockered to a sharp curve to make it easier for a player to turn and start quickly. Professional players also sharpen the blades before a game.

GLOVES

Gloves are made from leather, nylon, Kevlar, or a combination of these materials. Sizes range from 9 inches (23 cm) for youth hockey players to 16 inches (40 cm) for adults. Some players prefer a slightly larger fit for comfort, but the padding should cover the hand and wrist. Gloves should offer good protection for the thumb, fingers, and wrist, but be soft enough to let a player feel and grasp the stick. Some players prefer short gloves, but these should be worn with wrist guards.

PADDING

The hockey uniform is well-padded underneath. Shoulder pads protect the shoulders, collarbone, chest, back, and upper arms. An attached part adds rib protection.

Protective equipment is especially important for young players who are still growing. Here a coach tightens the boots of a player participating in the ten- to twelve-year age group.

Defensemen in the line of fire need larger pads. Additional pads are available to protect the heart area and lower back, coming as part of the shoulder pad or as an attachment. Attacking forwards wear lighter pads to offer more freedom of movement. Elbow pads, which can be adjusted with Velcro straps, should be long enough to cover from the shoulder pad to the glove. These protect against bruises and **fractures**. Some players add extra protection for their forearms by wearing what is called a forearm slash pad. Shin pads, which cover the kneecap and down to the boot top, are required, to guard against being struck by the puck or a stick. Again, defensemen wear heavier pads than forwards.

THE GOALTENDER

A goaltender is most often in the line of fire, the target of flying puck shots and powerful attackers. This explains why goalies look like astronauts about to step on the moon. Their protective equipment weighs as much as 40 pounds (18 kg) more than that of their teammates.

Shin guards are 4 inches (10 cm) thick or more, and are worn outside the socks to cover the leg from the thighs to the ankles. Padding for the shoulders, chests, and arms is also thicker.

The gloves for both hands are distinctive. The one on the hand holding the stick is called the "blocker glove" or "waffle pad" (in the game's early days, goalies used a rectangular pad with holes, which looked like a waffle). It is used to block shots and knock away the puck. The other glove is the "catching glove," used to scoop up the puck and toss it away from the goal.

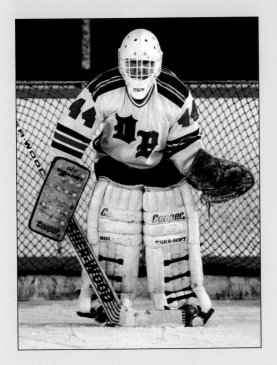

Boots are covered with molded plastic for extra protection. More of the boot's blade touches the ice to provide extra security.

A goalie can play his best because his equipment takes away most of the worry about serious injuries, letting him play boldly.

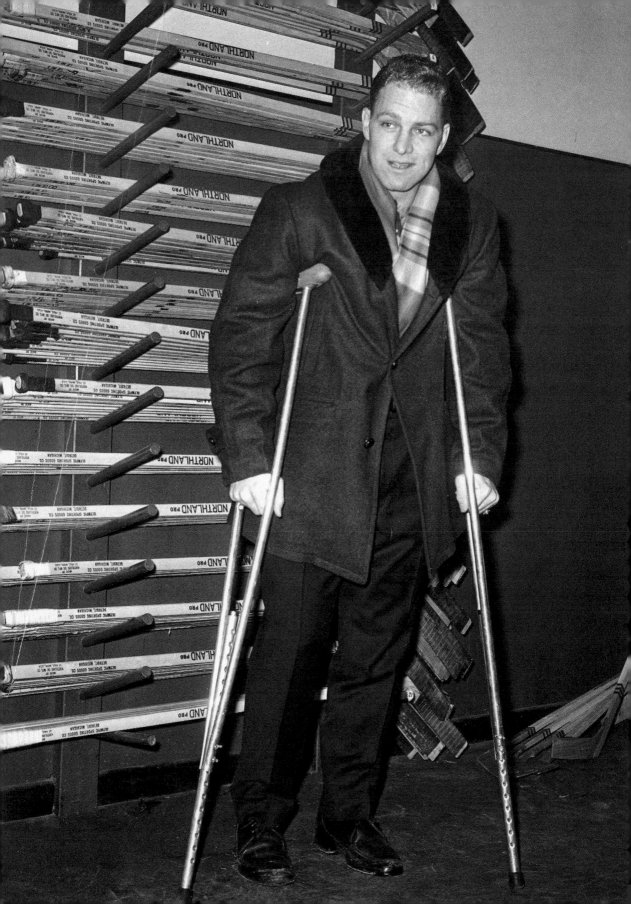

Injuries and Treatment

Hockey is a hard-hitting collision sport. Players regularly hit the ice and boards, or are hit by the speeding puck, swinging sticks, or even their opponents. And fighting does break out, especially at the professional level. Many players assume their protective equipment will keep them safe, but this assumption offers a false sense of security.

The most frequent hockey injuries are **contusions** and **lacerations**. The latter happen more often to the head and face, despite the use of helmets and face protectors. Muscle injuries are also common because hockey players must twist and turn constantly during games and keep their balance on the thin skates, putting great stress on the upper thigh, knee, and abdomen. Being hit by the puck can cause broken bones. Upper body injuries to the head, shoulders, arms, and hands are generally a result of falls and checking against the boards. Some estimates say one-third of all injuries are caused by illegal play.

About 80 percent of the above injuries are caused by a forceful impact and are variously called acute, acute traumatic, or direct trauma injuries. Another type is the **overuse**, or chronic, injury that happens because a player repeats the same motion over and over during a game and throughout the season. Fatigue also plays a part

Bobby Hull of the Chicago Black Hawks limped on crutches in 1963 after suffering a strained thigh, also called a "charley horse." Even minor injuries can keep players off the ice.

in this kind of injury. **Tendonitis**, the inflammation of a tendon in areas such as the knees and shoulders, is a typical injury caused by overuse and fatigue. An overuse injury is not as immediately serious as an acute one, but players should seek a physician's advice to ensure that it does not become worse as the season continues.

LEG AND FOOT BONES

Hockey players frequently suffer injuries in the area from the knee to the foot.

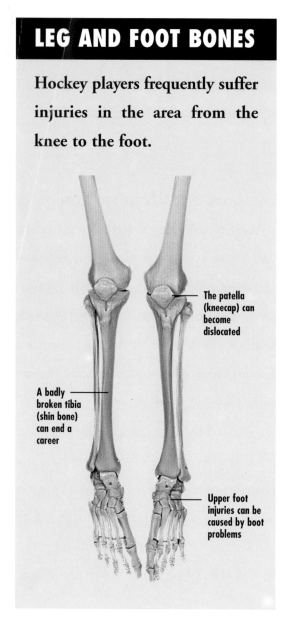

The patella (kneecap) can become dislocated

A badly broken tibia (shin bone) can end a career

Upper foot injuries can be caused by boot problems

FOOT AND ANKLE INJURIES

Even the slightest foot problem can be critical for a hockey player. This includes blisters that result from breaking in new boots. Bones in the foot and ankle can be fractured when hit by the puck or a stick, while ankle **sprains** result from the quick turns at high speeds.

Blisters are an irritating and painful problem that most players experience. Caused by the boot rubbing the foot, they generally form on the back of the heel, under the ball of the foot, and on the toes. Blisters often occur at the start of the season, but a player should try a new and better fitting boot if they occur regularly. Treatment generally involves a doughnut-shaped pad around the blister, a bandage, and over-the-counter medication. A blister should be kept clean to avoid infection when it breaks.

ONE TEAM'S INJURIES

To develop strategies for injury prevention, a research group at the University of Michigan Medical School in Ann Arbor studied the injuries suffered by twenty-two members of a Junior A hockey team, aged sixteen to twenty. They published their conclusions in the *Clinical Journal of Sports Medicine* in 1999:

- Goaltenders had the fewest injuries and forwards had the most.
- The face accounted for the most injuries, nearly 24 percent; next came shoulder, hand, and finger injuries; and finally knee and thigh injuries.
- Nearly 80 percent of injuries were contact injuries, including player collisions; stick and skate injuries; board, ice, and puck contact; fights.
- Players had more than twenty times as many injuries during games as during practices.
- Injuries happened more often in the later periods of games and during the latter part of each period, evidence that fatigue plays a role in causing injuries.
- The injury rate in the first half of the season was more than double that of the second half, implying that players became better conditioned with time.

Fractures, or broken bones, are common because a hockey player's feet receive many types of hits. Stress fractures are tiny cracks along a bone's surface, and are caused by repetitive stresses on the foot. The main symptom is pain, which increases as competition continues. If a fracture is suspected, a player should

Ankle sprains can result from simply turning on the ice. The most serious injuries to the ankle can require a six-week rest period, and the sprains will often recur.

immediately see a physician, who will take X-rays. The only real cure is rest, which requires sitting out a few games; young players usually heal faster than adults.

Ankle sprains involve overstretching the **ligaments** on the outside of the ankle and are accompanied by pain and swelling. The immediate treatment is to follow the **R.I.C.E.** program; the letters stand for "Rest, Ice, Compression, and Elevation."

As ankle sprains often recur, the rest period is important and may last from one to six weeks, depending on the seriousness of the tear. Ice will relieve the pain and swelling, and it should be applied for about twenty minutes at a time and repeated every two hours. If necessary, continue for seventy-two hours. An easy method is to put crushed ice in a plastic bag and then wrap it in a towel, as the ice should not directly touch the skin. Compression involves using an elastic bandage, making sure that it does not restrict circulation. A team trainer or physician will be knowledgeable about taping and may even decide on a brace to avoid reinjury. Elevating the ankle above the heart level will also reduce swelling.

After about three days, the ankle can be soaked in warm water for about fifteen minutes at a time to help restore mobility. Rehabilitation for the ankle can begin with light jogging, then build up to normal running.

LEG INJURIES

Hockey players often incur leg injuries in collisions with other players or the goal posts, boards, and ice. The lower leg takes most of the blows from the puck, and additional injuries come from the sticks and skates. These include bruises, muscle **strains**, and fractures.

Bruises, or contusions, on the leg or other areas of the body can rupture small blood vessels, causing blood to pool on the inside of the bruised muscle. The prime area for bruising is the **quadriceps**, the large muscle at the front of the thigh. The standard treatment to reduce the soreness and swelling is the R.I.C.E. program, especially the elevation of the leg to reduce a further collection of blood.

Muscle strains, also called pulls, involve a stretch or tear in a muscle, and are the result of constant twisting and turning at top speeds. Besides the leg, pulls often occur in the abdomen and pelvic areas. Sometimes they will be caused by a player not warming up enough or by being fatigued late in the game.

Strains and tears generally happen low in the quadriceps and high in the hamstrings, the three muscles at the back of the thigh. For these injuries, follow the R.I.C.E. program, and do light stretching exercises after three or four days, because this reduces the formation of scar tissue. The period of rest from hockey will be four weeks or longer. Fractures of the leg are rare but serious, as they can end a player's season. They normally occur from a fall or violent collision, and are accompanied by a sharp pain and severe swelling. The most endangered bones are in the lower leg: the large tibia, or shinbone, and the thin, outer fibula. Stress fractures from overuse are also common and will feel more like a generalized pain. It is best not to move the broken leg until medical help arrives, but a cold pack can be used to lessen the pain. Obviously, a broken leg must then be treated immediately by a physician, who will take X-rays and decide if splints or crutches are needed. The best treatment is rest.

THIGH MUSCLES

The large muscles in a hockey player's thighs can often be bruised, stretched, or torn.

The large iliopsoas muscle is the most powerful one in the thigh

The four quadricep muscles experience strains and tears

The rectus femoris flexes the knee joint

The strong quadriceps tendon goes into the top of the patella (kneecap)

KNEE INJURIES

Knee injuries are frequent in hockey, due to a player's turns and falls. The problems include tendinitis, sprains and strains, cartilage injuries, and a dislocated kneecap. Severe knee injuries can shorten a career.

Knee sprains happen when one or more ligaments are overstretched or torn. In hockey, this is usually the medial collateral ligament (M.C.L.), which is injured when a blow pushes the knee inward. You will hear a popping sound and feel deep pain. A strain is a partial

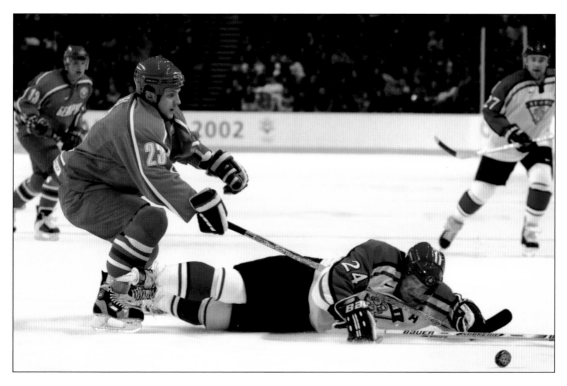

Many serious hockey injuries result from hard falls on the ice. Even if a player is one of the best in his league, the collisions and quick changes of direction can upset his balance.

or full tear of a muscle or tendon, and this has about the same feeling of discomfort as a sprain. For both, the R.I.C.E. program and several weeks of rest can be combined with the use of a splint or crutches. A knee sprain often requires surgery, especially if the hockey player is a professional or is considering a career playing the game.

A cartilage injury to the knee involves the softer material between bones. Young players are more likely to suffer from this injury. A hard blow to the knee, often from a fall or collision, injures the cartilage, some of which breaks away from the knee bone (patella) and causes swelling and pain. The knee will also lock, and the leg cannot be extended. About 30 percent of these injuries heal themselves, but surgery is often needed, followed by exercises, such as bicycle riding, to strengthen the knee muscles.

The kneecap, or patella, is the bone at the front of the knee inside the tendon that joins the quadriceps to the top of the tibia, or lower leg bone. A dislocated kneecap can occur when the knee is hit from the front or the inside of the kneecap, or when a player turns quickly and twists the thigh. These accidents knock the movable kneecap sideways. The area will swell and be painful, and the side of the knee usually develops a bulge. The R.I.C.E. treatment is used; a physician may reset the kneecap and recommend that the player wear a special brace.

KNEE

An unstable knee can be a source of problems for any hockey player.

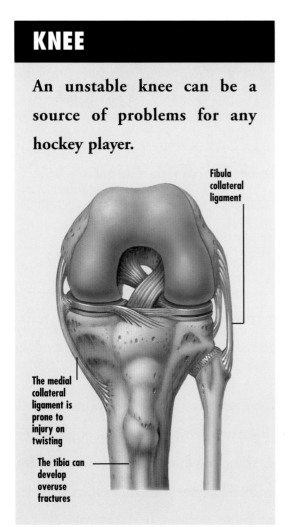

Fibula collateral ligament

The medial collateral ligament is prone to injury on twisting

The tibia can develop overuse fractures

SHOULDER INJURIES

Shoulder injuries are usually the result of overuse or hard blows. A hockey player can suffer from shoulder tendonitis, caused by constantly hitting the puck. The two main problems are separated and dislocated shoulders.

A separated shoulder involves the acromioclavicular (A.C.) joint, where the collar bone, or clavicle, joins the shoulder blade. Ligaments keep the joint together, but a blow can tear them, causing the collar bone to raise slightly. This is a painful injury. Most separations are treated with ice packs and healed by rest and strengthening exercises, but a very bad separation might require a physician to wire the joint together.

A dislocated shoulder is more serious because the head of the humerus bone pops out of its socket, usually toward the front. This is often caused by a fall or blow directly on the point of the shoulder, which tears cartilage. A doctor will take X rays, control the pain with medication, and may recommend wearing a shoulder sling for up to three weeks. Surgery is required for only the most serious dislocations.

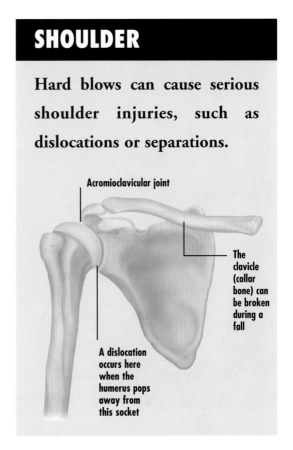

SHOULDER

Hard blows can cause serious shoulder injuries, such as dislocations or separations.

Acromioclavicular joint

The clavicle (collar bone) can be broken during a fall

A dislocation occurs here when the humerus pops away from this socket

HAND INJURIES

The hands, wrists, and fingers of hockey players can suffer normal and stress fractures, and sprains. Although falls are a prime cause, the irony is that many of these injuries occur when players remove their gloves to take part in a fight on the ice. The injured parts should be taped, with a splint, by the team trainer or a doctor.

HEAD AND FACE INJURIES

Most lacerations on the head and face can be bandaged and otherwise treated by team trainers with very little lost playing time. Concussions, however, can be a serious matter requiring special attention.

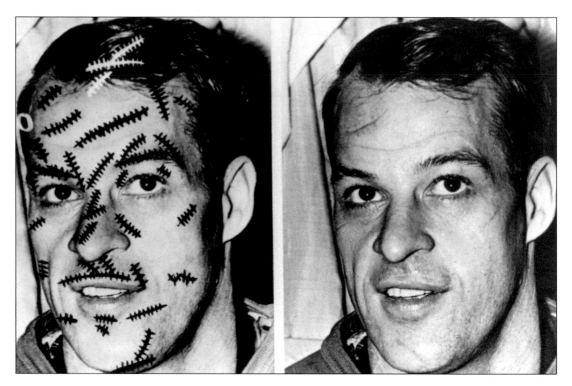

With the help of the artist's brush, Detroit Red Wings' Gordie Howe is shown with every facial cut he has suffered in fourteen years of play in the big leagues. His injuries included a skull fracture (circle) and 200 head stitches.

A concussion may result from a hard fall on the ice. In most cases, the injury will be fairly mild, and the player will suffer from a headache, light-headedness, poor balance, and a lack of alertness. Sometimes a player may have slight **amnesia** or even be unconscious for a short period. If this happens, the player should stop playing immediately. Never underestimate such a head injury: there is a chance that a hard blow can create pressure and bleeding under the skull, which can develop into a fatal hematoma. A physician will therefore take X-rays and scans, and the player will have to rest from hockey for a period of a week to a month after the symptoms disappear. The NHL uses neuropsychological testing to ensure that players who suffered from concussions do not return to the ice while still at risk.

RETURNING TO PLAY

One of the most frustrating things about an injury is having to sit out games while recovering. Almost any injury, from a sprained ankle to a concussion, may recur if a hockey player returns to the ice sooner than is recommended. The rehabilitation period may be from several weeks to six months.

It is important to follow the physician's advice on medication or physical aids, her directions regarding an exercise program or physical therapy, and her recommendations on adjusting the level of play and wearing protective devices. Even after a full rehabilitation period, a player may find that the injured area has started to hurt again during a game. If so, the player should leave the ice immediately and tell both the coach and physician.

NECK INJURIES

Minor neck injuries include a sprain or strain, such as whiplash, in which the neck is snapped back during play, or "stingers," in which the nerves of the neck are stretched, causing a stinging pain and temporary numbness. Such a serious injury as a neck fracture may involve the spinal cord, and this can result in paralysis or even death. For this reason, an injured player on the ground who has a suspected neck injury should not be moved until an emergency crew arrives. This rule also applies to an unconscious player, who might have both a head and neck injury. Most cases, however, are not severe and require only a rest from the game and a possible neck brace until the muscles are strengthened by exercise.

Careers in Hockey

The road to a career in professional hockey could well begin at the age of five, and there are many opportunities available for those who want to learn and play the game.

U.S.A. Hockey, Inc., the national governing body for the sport, oversees teams for players aged six and under (totaling 42,719 players in the 2001–2002 season), as well as youth teams, which are divided by age into divisions called Mites, Squirts, Pee Wees, Bantams, and Midgets. All leagues are well organized and must use approved protective equipment and meet certain standards of behavior on the ice.

Training is available at many local hockey schools and camps. In 2003, the annual U.S.A. Hockey Summer Camp in Ann Arbor, Michigan, received $20,000 from the new NHL Diversity Hockey Scholarship Program in order to help economically disadvantaged boys and girls of all ages in the United States play the game.

Many annual championships are also available for players of different ages, with the International Youth Hockey Tournaments hosting 1,800 teams with 60,000 players for the 2001–2002 season.

The joy of victory belongs to Mario Lemieux, captain of the Pittsburgh Penguins, as he holds up the Stanley Cup after his team downed Minnesota for the NHL championship in 1991.

THE COLLEGE GAME

Hockey, once confined to the cold climates of Canada and some American states, has taken advantage of modern arenas to expand into high schools and colleges throughout the warmer states. Indeed, the University of Alabama at Huntsville won the National Collegiate Athletic Association's (NCAA) Division II National Championship in 1996 and 1998. The North still dominates the college sport, with six major conferences: the Central Collegiate Hockey Association, Eastern Collegiate Athletic Conference, College Hockey America, Hockey East Association, Metro Atlantic Athletic Conference, and Western Collegiate Hockey Association. The NCAA's annual championship comes down to the playoffs of the "Frozen Four" top teams, and the final game of the 2002 championships drew a record 2,319,420 television viewers.

The names of NCAA divisional tournament winners form a good list that high

Teamwork is one of the important principles taught in youth hockey leagues. Teammates can advance together through the many levels of the game.

One of a player's proudest moments is representing his country at the Winter Olympics. This face-off is between Canada and the United States, at the 1998 Winter Olympic Games in Nagano, Japan.

school players who wish to continue their game, possibly into the professional ranks, can study. The Division I championship has been won nine times by the University of Michigan; seven times by the University of North Dakota; five times by the University of Denver and the University of Washington; four times by Boston University; three times by Lake Superior State University (Michigan), Michigan Technological University, and the University of Minnesota; and twice

High school players huddle on the ice during the Minnesota state playoffs in St. Paul. Competitions such as this give players a chance to attract interest from colleges.

by Colorado College, Cornell University, the University of Maine, Michigan State University, and Rensselaer Polytechnic Institute (New York).

The Division II championship was discontinued in 1999. Its top winners were

Bemidji State University (Minnesota), which won five titles, and the University of Massachusetts at Lowell, which won three. The most championships won in Division III have been five by Middlebury College (Vermont) and two by Plattsburgh State University (New York). The University of Minnesota at Duluth won the NCAA Women's Championship in 2003 for the third consecutive time.

NATIONAL HOCKEY LEAGUE TEAMS

EASTERN CONFERENCE	WESTERN CONFERENCE
Atlanta Thrashers	Anaheim Mighty Ducks
Boston Bruins	Calgary Flames
Buffalo Sabres	Chicago Blackhawks
Carolina Hurricanes	Colorado Avalanche
Florida Panthers	Columbus Blue Jackets
Montreal Canadiens	Dallas Stars
New Jersey Devils	Detroit Red Wings
New York Islanders	Edmonton Oilers
New York Rangers	Los Angeles Kings
Ottawa Senators	Minnesota Wild
Philadelphia Flyers	Nashville Predators
Pittsburgh Penguins	Phoenix Coyotes
Tampa Bay Lightning	San Jose Sharks
Toronto Maple Leafs	St. Louis Blues
Washington Capitals	Vancouver Canucks

LIKE FATHER, LIKE SON

Bobby Hull (1939–) scored 610 goals in 1,063 games in sixteen NHL seasons (1957–1972) at left wing with the Chicago Black Hawks. A Hockey Hall of Famer, he is acknowledged as one of the greats of the game. However, his son Brett bettered that total at right wing, scoring his 611th goal in the first game of the 2000–2001 season with the Dallas Stars and his 700th on February 10, 2003, with the Detroit Red Wings, becoming only the sixth player in NHL history to reach that mark.

Bobby Hull led the NHL in scoring seven times, but his team won the Stanley Cup only once (1961). Nicknamed "the Golden Jet" because of his blond hair, he was known for his fair play, which won him the Lady Byng Trophy for good sportsmanship in 1966. His son Brett, nicknamed "the Golden Brett," was traded to the St. Louis Blues in 1987, scoring 527 goals in his ten seasons there. In 1999, he clinched the Stanley Cup for Dallas in triple overtime against Buffalo, and in 2001 he helped Detroit win the Stanley Cup.

Brett Hull skated into the record books when he bettered the goal record of his famous father, Bobby.

PLAYING PROFESSIONALLY

Many college players who are not drafted into the NHL have found satisfying careers with minor league hockey teams, and some then move up to the NHL. The top minor league is the American Hockey League, which was established in 1936. It has twenty-eight teams, and all but two have a direct working agreement with an NHL team. The East Coast Hockey League has twenty-seven widespread teams, such as the Atlantic City Boardwalk Bullies, Louisiana Ice Gators, and Toledo Storm. Established in 1988, it sent 192 former players to the NHL by 2003. It absorbed the six-team West Coast Hockey League for the 2003–2004 season, and new franchises scheduled for the future will bring the expanded league to forty teams.

Many smaller minor leagues, such as the United Hockey League, which fielded ten teams from the Great Lakes region through New York State for the 2002–2003 season, also offer opportunities for advancement.

Although a player must be eighteen to be picked in the NHL draft, some as young as fourteen have been approached by agents wanting to represent them. Any high school player who signs with an agent, however, becomes ineligible to play at an NCAA college. The NHL draft is held in June each year. Teams that do not make the playoffs have the first selections from the draft, and any expansion clubs are added to this group. The order of draw is selected by a lottery. The teams that made the playoffs then choose players in reverse order, with the last-place team choosing first.

An NHL career can indeed be financially rewarding: Sergei Fedorov of the Detroit Red Wings received a $12 million bonus during the 1997–1998 season, and Eric Lindros signed a $37 million ten-year contract with the New York Rangers in 2001.

CHRONOLOGY OF HOCKEY

1853: First hockey game played with a disk, which replaced the ball used in bandy.

1879: First rules drawn up by two McGill University students.

1908: The International Ice Hockey Federation (IIHF) established.

1917: National Hockey League (NHL) founded as an outgrowth of the National Hockey Association.

1920: Hockey played as a demonstration sport at the Olympics.

1923: Hart Trophy for the NHL player "most useful to his club" first awarded.

1926: Vezina Trophy for the NHL goaltender allowing the fewest number of goals first awarded.

1930: First World Hockey Championship tournament played.

1936: Calder Memorial Trophy for the NHL's outstanding rookie first awarded.

1943: The Hockey Hall of Fame established in Toronto.

1947: Annual NHL All-Star Game first played; Art Ross Trophy first awarded to NHL's leading scorer.

1967: NHL expands from six to twelve teams.

1981: The Hobey Baker Award for college hockey's Player of the Year first presented.

1990: First Women's World Hockey Championship tournament played.

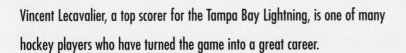

Vincent Lecavalier, a top scorer for the Tampa Bay Lightning, is one of many hockey players who have turned the game into a great career.

Glossary

Aerobic: Used to describe exercise that demands increased oxygen, thereby increasing the heart rate and breathing.

Amnesia: Loss of memory.

Cardiovascular: Relating to the heart and lungs.

Cartilage: Strong connective tissue found in the body's joints and other structures. Children have a higher percentage of cartilage than adults. Some of it turns to bone as children grow older.

Concussion: A serious injury to the brain caused by a hard blow to the head.

Contusion: The medical name for a bruise; the skin is not broken.

Diuretic: Any substance that helps remove water from the body by increasing the flow of urine.

Fracture: A crack, break, or shattering of a bone.

Hamstrings: The group of three large muscles set at the back of the thigh.

Laceration: The medical name for a cut deep enough to require stitches.

Ligament: A short band of tough body tissue, which connects bones or holds together joints.

Overuse injury: A chronic injury that happens because a player repeats the same motion over and over during a game and throughout the season.

Puck: The rubber disk, 3 inches (7.5 cm) in diameter, which the players shoot at the goal.

Quadriceps: A large four-part muscle on the front of the thigh, used to extend the leg.

R.I.C.E.: An injury treatment program of rest, ice, compression, and elevation.

Sprain: A stretch or tear of a ligament.

Strain: A stretch or tear of a muscle or tendon.

Tendonitis: Inflammation and pain in the tendons.

Tendon: A body tissue, also called a sinew, that connects muscles to bones.

Visualization: The technique of improving sports performance by imagining yourself playing well.

Further Information

USEFUL WEB SITES

International Ice Hockey Federation: www.iihf.com

National Collegiate Athletic Association (NCAA): www.ncaa.org

National Hockey League: www.nhl.com

U.S.A. Hockey: www.usahockey.com

To find out about mental imagery, see:

www.whyfiles.org/019olympic/sport_psych1.html

The Web sites listed on this page were active at the time of publication. The publisher is not responsible for Web sites that have changed their address or discontinued operation since the date of publication. The publisher will review and update the Web sites upon each reprint.

FURTHER READING

Brill, Marlene Targ. *Winning Women in Ice Hockey*. Hauppauge, New York: Barron's Juveniles, 1999.

Gutman, Bill. *Ice Hockey: Start Right and Play Well*. Lakeville, Connecticut: Grey Castle Press, 1990.

Kalb, Jonah. *The Easy Hockey Book*. Boston: Houghton Mifflin, 1977.

Kennedy, Mike. *Ice Hockey*. New York: Franklin Watts, 2003.

Stewart, Mark. *Hockey: A History of the Fastest Game on Ice*. New York: Franklin Watts, 1999.

_____*Mario Lemieux: Own the Ice*. Brookfield, Connecticut: Millbrook Press, 2002.

THE AUTHOR

Dr. John D. Wright is a writer and journalist with many years of experience. He has been a reporter for *Time* and *People* magazines, a journalist for the U.S. Navy, and reported for newspapers in Alabama and Tennessee. He holds a Ph.D. degree in Communications from the University of Texas, and has taught journalism at colleges in Alabama and Virginia. He now lives in Herefordshire, England.

THE CONSULTANTS

Susan Saliba, Ph.D., is a senior associate athletic trainer and a clinical instructor at the University of Virginia in Charlottesville, Virginia. A certified athletic trainer and licensed physical therapist, Dr. Saliba provides sports medicine care, including prevention, treatment, and rehabilitation for the varsity athletes at the University. Dr. Saliba holds dual appointments as an Assistant Professor in the Curry School of Education and the Department of Orthopaedic Surgery. She is a member of the National Athletic Trainers' Association's Educational Executive Committee and its Clinical Education Committee.

Eric Small, M.D., a Harvard-trained sports medicine physician, is a nationally recognized expert in the field of sports injuries, nutritional supplements, and weight management programs. He is author of *Kids & Sports* (2002) and is Assistant Clinical Professor of Pediatrics, Orthopedics, and Rehabilitation Medicine at Mount Sinai School of Medicine in New York. He is also Director of the Sports Medicine Center for Young Athletes at Blythedale Children's Hospital in Valhalla, New York. Dr. Small has served on the American Academy of Pediatrics Committee on Sports Medicine for the past six years, where he develops national policy regarding children's medical issues and sports.

Index

Page numbers in *italics* refer to photographs and illustrations.

ankle injuries 40, 42–3

bandy 9, 13, 58
boots 34, *35*, *36*, 37, 40
Boston Bruins 13, 55

Canada 13, 14, 15, 52
Chicago Black Hawks 13, *38*, 55, 56
colleges 12, 52–5, 59

Dallas Stars 55, 56
dehydration 28–9
Detroit Red Wings 11, 13, *48*, 55, 56, 57
diet 27–9
doctors 42, 43, 44, 47, 48, 49

Edmonton Oilers 15, 55
equipment
    boots 34, *35*, *36*, 37, 40
    face masks *32*, 33–4, 39
    gloves *34*, 35, 37, 47
    helmets *32*, 33, 39
    mouth guards 34
    padding *34*, 35–6, 37
    skates *35*, 37
exercises
    conditioning 27, 29
    warm-ups *24*, 25–7, 29
    see also muscles; preparation

face injuries 39, 41, 47–8
face masks *32*, 33–4, 39
face-offs *8*, 16, 23
falls 39, 41, 44, *45*, 48 *see also* injuries
foot and ankle injuries 40–3
fractures 39, 40–2, 44

gloves *34*, 35, 37, 47
goaltenders *32*, 37, 41, 57
Gretzky, Wayne 15

hand injuries 39, 47
Hart Trophy 11, 58
head injuries 11, 39, 41, 47–8
helmets *32*, 33, 39
Hockey Hall of Fame 14, 15, 56, 59

Howe, Gordie 11, *48*
Hull, Bobby *38*, 56
Hull, Brett *24*, 56

ice hockey
    history 9–10, 12–14, 58–9
    rules 9, 13, 16–17, 58
    tactics 21
    terms 21, 23
    worldwide appeal 13–14
injuries
    ankles 40, 42–3
    dislocations 46, 47
    feet 40–2
    fractures 39, 40–2, 44
    hands 39, 47
    head and face 11, 39, 41, 47–8
    impact 39, 41, 46
    knees 44–6
    legs *38*, 43–4
    overuse 39–40, 46
    R.I.C.E. treatment 42–3, 45, 46
    shoulders 39, 41, 46–7
    sprains 40, 42–3, 45, 47, 49
    tendonitis 40, 44, 46
International Ice Hockey Federation
    (IIHF) 13, 58

knee injuries 44–6

leg injuries *38*, 43–4
Lemieux, Mario *50*

McGill University Hockey Club 10, 58
mental preparation *18*, 19–20, 22
muscles
    developing 27, 29
    hamstrings 31, 43
    quadriceps 43, *44*
    stretching *24*, 25–7, 29, 30–1

National Collegiate Athletic Association
    (NCAA) 52–5, 57
National Hockey League (NHL) 12–13,
    15, 51, 55, 56, 57, 58–9
New York Rangers 13, 55, 57

Olympic Games *12*, 13–14, *22*, *53*, 58
overuse injuries 39–40, 46

padding *34*, 35–6, 37
pain 41, 44, 46, 47, 49
physical preparation *24*, 25–31
Pittsburgh Penguins *50*, 55
players 9, 16
positive thinking *18*, 19–20, 22
preparation
    mental *18*, 19–20, 22
    physical *24*, 25–31
professional players 12–13, 57
protective equipment *32*, 33–7

referees *8*, 17
Rest, Ice, Compression and Elevation
    (R.I.C.E.) treatment 42–3, 45, 46
rinks 13, 16
rules 9, 13, 16–17, 58

self-confidence *18*, 19–20, 22
shoulder injuries 39, 41, 46–7
skates *35*, 37
sledge hockey 22
sprains 40, 42–3, 45, 47, 49
St. Louis Blues *24*, 55, 56
Stanley Cup 10, 13, *50*, 56
stretching *24*, 25–7, 29, 30–1

tendonitis 40, 44, 46
terminology 21, 23
Toronto Maple Leafs 13, 55
training camps 51
    see also exercises; preparation

U.S.A. Hockey Inc. 51
universities 12, 52–5, 59

visualization *18*, 19–20, 22

warm-ups *24*, 25–7, 29
World Hockey Association 15